TRANSITIONS

TRANSITIONS

The Challenge of Change

Dr Barrie Hopson,
Mike Scally and Kevern Stafford

MERCURY

First published in 1988 by Lifeskills Publishing Group
New Edition published in 1992
by Mercury Books
Gold Arrow Publications Ltd
862 Garratt Lane, London SW17 0NB

Drawings by Kate Charlesworth

Typeset by Phoenix Photosetting, Chatham, Kent

Printed and bound in Great Britain by
Mackays of Chatham PLC, Chatham, Kent

British Library Cataloguing in Publication Data is available

ISBN 1–85252–120–1

Foreword

Dear Reader,

Welcome to our series of open learning workbooks! In this brief foreword, we invite you to consider some of our beliefs:

- We do not need teachers to learn! Most of what we know in life was not learned in school, college or formal education. We can, and do, learn in a whole range of ways and we learn best when we know our own needs.

- The best way to help people is to encourage them to help themselves. Self-help and self-management avoid the dependency which blocks development and burdens ourselves and others.

- Awareness, knowledge and skills give us more options in life. Lack of any of these is a disadvantage; possession of them allows us to live fuller lives, shaping events rather than simply reacting.

- The more able and accomplished we become, the more we fill society's reservoir of talent and contribute to the common good.

The term 'lifeskill' came from work based on these beliefs which we began at Leeds University in the 1970s. Our philosophy has been widely applied in education, in industry and commerce, and in the community, inviting people to take charge of their lives and make them satisfying and rewarding.

Lifeskills have so far been available through training courses and teaching programmes. *Now* they are available in a self-help format consistent with the Lifeskills approach because *you* are in charge of your own learning. Learn at your own pace, in your own time, and apply your learning to your situation. We wish you both enjoyment and success!

Barrie Hopson

Mike Scally

November 1991

Before You Start...

This workbook has been written for people wanting to know more about personal self-development. It is about reading and doing, so we have chosen to write it as an open learning workbook.

What is open learning? Open learning is a term used to describe a study programme which is very flexibly designed so that it adapts to the needs of individual learners. Some open learning programmes involve attendance at a study centre of some kind, or contact with a tutor or mentor, but even then attendance times are flexible and suit the individual. This workbook is for you to use at home or at work and most of the activities are for you to complete alone. We sometimes suggest that it would be helpful to talk with a friend or colleague – self development is easier if there is another person with whom to talk over ideas. But this isn't essential by any means.

With this workbook you can:

- organise your study to suit your own needs.

- study the material alone or with other people

- work through the book at your own pace

- start and finish just where and when you want to, although we have indicated some suggested stopping points with a ☕ symbol.

The sections marked Personal Project involve you in more than working through the text. They require you to take additional time – sometimes an evening, sometimes a week. For this reason, we are not giving clear guidelines on how long it will take you to complete this workbook, but the written part of the book will probably take you about six hours to complete.

Contents

Introduction: Metamorphosis

Metamorphosis means change from one thing to something else. It can involve a change of appearance, condition, character or situation. You have metamorphosed into the person you are today. You are the product of thousands, maybe millions, of changes: some small, some large. Some you don't even notice, some are a shock!

Another word for change is transition – a period of change. This book will help you to cope with transitions and change by helping you to understand your own thoughts and feelings about it. By working through the book at your own pace, you will be able to develop new skills so that, when you are faced with major changes, or when you do not achieve the hoped for change in your life, you will be better able to understand the stages of a transition and its likely effect on you.

Any change can be exciting; it can also be confusing and worrying.

This book will enable you to do the following:

You will:

1)   be able to recognise the two types of transition

2)   know the seven stages of a transition

3)   understand when you are approaching and going through a major life transition

4)   appreciate the stress and potential upset involved in going through a transition

5)   develop your own skills and acquire additional strategies to help you and others manage transitions well

6)   appreciate the positive side of transitions: that they present opportunities for personal growth and development.

Use the space below to note down any of these objectives which you might find particularly useful. Add any of your own if they are different; what do you hope to gain from completing this book?

....

....

....

....

....

You might find it useful to refer back to these notes occasionally as you work through the book. You can keep a check on whether you really are developing the skills you want, and keep yourself on course.

Section One: Transitions – Why Learn About Them?

In this section we will look at what a transition is and what the two types of transition are. You will also have the opportunity to think about some of the transitions you have experienced in the past. We begin by offering you a selection of definitions:

> **transition** – Passage from one state or action or subject or set of circumstances to another; period during which one style is developing into another.
> *Pocket Oxford Dictionary*

> 'You may suddenly feel that it is all too much hard work and that you cannot go on and would like to go home and forget about having a baby. Or you may become irritable with everyone around you and hypercritical of the help your partner is giving.'
> *Sheila Kitzinger writing about the transition stage of labour in* Pregnancy and Childbirth *(1980)*

> 'In the ongoing flux of life, man undergoes many changes. Arriving, departing, growing, declining, achieving, failing – every change involves a loss and a gain. The old environment must be given up, the new accepted. People come and go, one job is lost, another begun; territory and possessions are acquired or sold; new skills are learned, old abandoned; expectations are fulfilled or hopes dashed – in all these situations the individual is faced with the need to give up one mode of life and accept another.'
> *A psychologist's definition – C M Parkes (1972)*

Using the information and examples we have given you so far, use this space to write down your own working definition of a transition. Feel free to use parts of the above quotes. Does anything else come to mind? a poem? an incident? If so, incorporate them into your definition.

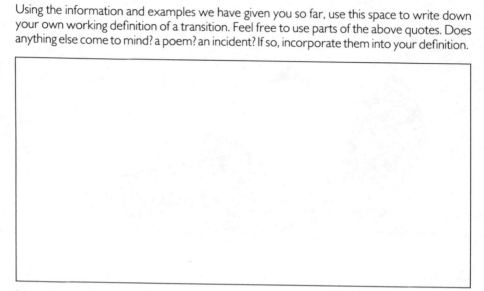

Now that you have begun to think about what a transition is, we will go on to look more specifically at different kinds of transition.

The Two Types of Transition

There are two major types of transition which we all have to cope with:

1)   stages of personal development

2)   major life events.

Let's look at them in more detail.

1)   Stages of Personal Development

Roger Gould (1978)*, observed that in children the passing of years is marked by their changing bodies, while in adults it is marked by changes in mental attitude. His work led him to define seven stages of adult life and what is likely to happen to the individual during each stage.

We reproduce for you here these Seven Stages of Personal Development. As you read through them, try to remember what your life was like at these ages. Can you identify when the stages began and ended? Are there any you haven't yet reached?

---

*Gould R.L. (1978) *Transformations: Growth & Change in Adult Life*, Simon & Schuster.

Stages	Features
1) Pulling up roots (late teens early 20s)	Autonomy Self-sufficiency
2) Provisional adulthood (20s)	Select a career Establish personal relationships Achieve a place in society
3) Age 30 transition (late 20s early 30s)	Search for personal identity Reassess future objectives Search for meaning in life
4) Rooting (30s)	Establish long-term goals Receive recognition in career Career success
5) Mid-life transition (late 30s early to mid 40s)	Confrontation of gap between achievement & aspirations Re-examination of career Re-examination of personal relationships
6) Re-establishment & flowering (mid 40s to 50s)	Acceptance of time as finite Confrontation of mortality Greater autonomy
7) Mellowing (50s–60s)	Acceptance of 'I own myself' Fewer personal relationships Examination of present & what it means

Write down in the space below anything you feel about any of the stages.

You might feel happy and satisfied with your achievements, or you may find that you feel dissatisfied with how parts of your life have gone so far. Try to remember that none of your experiences are ever wasted; they all go to make you uniquely *you*.

The ages we have used are approximate, but what the table shows is that transitions occur throughout our lives. As a child or teenager you probably thought adulthood and being 'grown up' meant being stable, set in your ways and knowing all the answers. This is rarely the case. Are you the same now as you were ten years ago? Do you expect or want to be the same ten years hence?

Think back ten years and fill in some of these details:

What did you wear?

....

....

What did you do during the day?

....

....

What did you do with your free time?

....

....

What was your favourite music/TV/film?

....

....

Who were your closest friends/family?

....

....

What was your income?

....

Back to the present, answer the same questions for now:

What do you wear?

....

....

What do you do during the day?

....

....

What do you do with your free time?

....

....

What is your favourite music/TV/film?

....

....

Who are your closest friends/family?

....

....

What is your income?

....

Are the two lists different? In what way? Jot down your thoughts here:

....

....

....

Having looked at the differences between you as you are now and you as you were ten years ago, how do you feel about those changes? You can use this space to make a note of good or bad feelings about the ways you have changed.

....

....

....

....

Perhaps some things have stayed the same. Are there some similarities between the two lists? Use this space to make a note of these.

....

....

....

....

How do you feel about the similarities between now and then? Use this space to make a note of your good or bad feelings.

....

....

....

....

Now spend a moment thinking about:

• how you expect to be in ten years' time

• how you would like to be in ten years' time

It's good to take time to think about what you want, then you can plan to achieve it. You can use this space to make a note of what you expect or hope to have achieved in ten years' time.

....

....

....

....

....

You may have found that task quite challenging. We can imagine how we *might* be in the future, but we don't know for sure. We can't know because we have no idea how we will change or what will happen to us. Which brings us on to the next type of transition.

2)   Major Life Events, Challenge & Stress

Does it ever end? You've barely got used to life in the womb when you're pushed into the outside world. That's OK, but then there's school (40,000 hours altogether), perhaps your parents move house or split up, friends and relatives come and go, you're an adolescent, your body changes, boyfriends, girlfriends, exams, college, work, unemployment, marriage, partner for life, divorce, flats, houses, new job, new town; and so on until we make the greatest transition of all (unfortunately we can't tell you much about what happens after that one).

Life is a series of challenges for us all – whether we like it or not!

Some people enjoy stability, some prefer to be always on the move – you will have the opportunity to think more about this later on in the book. But whoever you are, it is inevitable that you will be faced with major life events and, consciously or unconsciously, they will almost certainly be a stimulus or a shock to the system.

These challenges in our lives can be seen positively, as something to be enjoyed, experienced and learned from; or negatively, as something daunting that you'd rather not face. They all represent periods of transition in life. Think of some challenges you have faced positively, where you feel you have coped well. (A challenge can be any event where you have had to prove yourself – it doesn't mean climbing Everest!)

Five challenges I have faced positively:

1. ....

2. ....

3. ....

4. ....

5. ....

Is there a theme which links all or most of these challenges? What is it?

....

....

Now make a list of the five most worrying or stressful things that have happened to you. Stressful events are not necessarily bad. Getting married, for instance, is one of the most stressful events known to man, woman, mother-in-law and father of the bride!

Times of stress in my life:

1. ....

2. ....

3. ....

4. ....

5. ....

Once again, is there a theme which links all or most of these events? What is it?

....

....

Did any of your positive challenges reappear on your stressful list? If so, why do you think that is?

....

....

It is likely that most of your challenges and stressful events were transitions. Go back to page 12 and re-read your own definition of a transition, then go through the two lists you have just made, and tick the events which fit that definition.

Take a look at these statistics on stress levels. The life events are all transitions, and it is more than likely that you will have a number of them on your two lists.

Important Life Events and how Stressful they are for Adults*

Life Event	Score out of 100
Death of wife or husband	100
Divorce	73
Separation	65
Going to prison	63
Death of a close family member	63
Personal injury or illness	53
Getting married	50
Losing your job	47
A separated couple getting together again	45
Retirement	45
A change in health of a close family member	44
Pregnancy	40

*Holmes T.H. and Rahe R.H. (1967)

While these are regarded as highly stressful events in our lives, you will notice that some can also be occasions of great happiness – pregnancy, marriage or getting together again after a separation, for example. Have you experienced any of these important life events? Are you about to face one of these major life challenges? You can use this space if you would like to note down your thoughts and feelings about this list.

....

....

....

....

....

Summary

In this section we have identified what a transition is. We have seen that a transition can be a stage in our personal development, or it can be a major change or challenge in our lives. You have looked back over your own life and found your own transition stages and challenges that you overcame. In the next section, we will go on to look at the transition process in more detail.

Most people are aware of the problems associated with being overstressed: it is bad for our health, it prevents us from functioning well, it makes us unhappy. However, a certain level of stress is inevitable and, more importantly, it is valuable. It makes us perform well; it gets our adrenalin flowing when we need it. You can't climb Everest without a high level of productive stress!

There are a number of techniques which will help you cope with stress, but understanding transitions will make emergency stress management techniques less necessary. Understanding that major changes in our lives, whether they are the result of events or of personal development, are natural, and developing skills to cope with them can minimise stress. We will then be better able to respond to the challenge of change.

Section Two: The Seven Stages of Transition

A vital part of dealing with any problem is to *know* the problem. Hopefully, you already know what a transition is; we are now going to break that down further so you can recognise the stages of a transition. Knowing where you are in a transition, knowing that your feelings will pass (and knowing that your feelings are so normal that you've read about them in a book!) will help you control what is happening and move through the transition easily. We have divided these feelings into seven stages.

The seven stages can be seen on the graph on page 22, which shows how your feelings about yourself might change over the course of a transition. As the graph shows, your self-esteem will rise and fall as you move through the seven stages of transition. To give you some idea of how this might affect you, compare how you feel about yourself on a good day and on a bad day.

Transition and Your Self-Esteem

Your self-esteem is very important to how you feel. It can be described as how you rate yourself – or your feelings of self-worth. This can be influenced by all sorts of things: how you feel physically (if you are well or run-down); how things are going at work and in your daily life; how other people are responding to you.

On a good day

These are the days when everything goes swimmingly. Family and friends are co-operative and show their appreciation of you. At work, or in your daily activity, you rise to new challenges and enjoy them. You feel good about yourself, as though you could take on anything. And because you feel so strong and positive, it is as if you create your own luck: everything goes well for you. Again, our situation and the people around us contribute to our sense of self-worth.

Think of a time when you have experienced these feelings of self-worth. Try to pinpoint one or more reasons for your good feelings about yourself.

....

....

....

On a bad day

These are the days when nothing goes right. Your family are at odds with you, you feel tired and less able to cope. Perhaps you are being asked to do more than is reasonable, at work or in your daily activity. And because you are trying to do too much, you become increasingly tired and suffer feelings of helplessness. The more powerless you feel to change the situation, the more your own self-esteem suffers. If it goes on too long, you can end up feeling worthless – as if it is all your own fault, when really it is the situation that has affected your view of yourself.

Can you think of an occasion when you have felt like this? Can you pinpoint one or more things which contributed to your feelings about yourself at the time?

....

....

....

These feelings of high and low self-esteem (which everyone experiences) are shown on the left side of the graph on the next page. Look at the graph itself. The line showing self-esteem starts at the mid-point and then rises and falls as it passes through the seven stages of transition. These stages are explained fully after the graph.

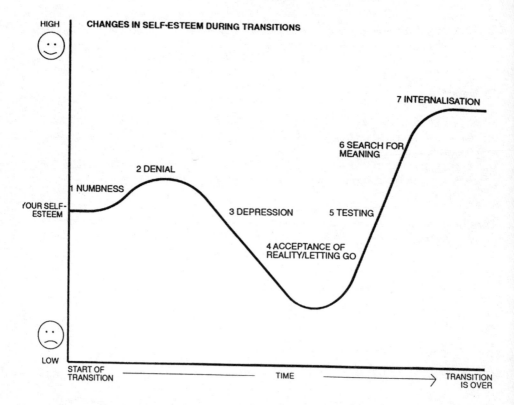

The Seven Stages: What are they? What do they mean?
=====

What you'll read next is our explanation of each of the seven stages. After reading each explanation, try to recall occasions when you have felt like that.

1   Numbness

The first phase is largely characterised by shock. It is a kind of immobilisation or a sense of being overwhelmed: of being unable to make plans, unable to reason, and unable to under-stand. In other words, you freeze up. The more unfamiliar the transition, the stronger the sense of immobilisation. In bereavement, for example, many people feel strange because of the absence of feeling; but it is normal to feel numb at this stage. However, if you feel positive about the transition, as you might feel positive about getting married, this stage will be less intense.

'Oh, no! I can't believe it!' Have I felt like this? When?

....

....

2   Minimisation/Denial

The movement from numbness to the second stage of denial does not feel greatly different at the time it is happening. This is because it is characterised by minimisation of the change or disruption, even by trivialising it. Very often we will attempt to deny that the change even exists! Sometimes people project feelings of euphoria; great if you've got a new job or a new baby, maybe less appropriate if you've just been sacked!

During this stage people may feel 'This is not as bad as I expected'. However, the apparent ease of the transition is because the body is building up its defences for the full impact of the transition which is yet to come. This is often a high energy stage because with a transition like bereavement the person is often at the centre of attention from their friends and relatives. With a transition such as promotion, the denial stage may be a refusal to recognise some of the real changes that will take place, for example the loss of workmates, new responsibilities and the uncertainty about being able to do the new job.

'This is not as bad as I expected' Have I felt like this? When?

....

....

3   Self-Doubt or Depression

Eventually, for most people, the realities of the change and of the resulting stress begin to become apparent. As people become aware that they must make some changes in the way they are living, as they become aware of the realities involved, they sometimes become uncertain. Self-doubt is usually a consequence of feelings of powerlessness, of aspects of life being out of our control. This can happen even when the transition is eagerly anticipated, not only when it is feared. So, a longed-for promotion can lead to grave doubts about being capable of doing the job.

This stage has occasional high energy periods, often characterised by anger, before sliding back into a feeling of hopelessness. We may become frustrated because it seems difficult to know how best to cope with the new life requirements, the new ways of being, the new relationships that have been established.

'I am not sure if I'm up to it' Have I felt like this? When?

....

....

4   Acceptance of Reality/Letting Go

As people gradually become aware of their new reality, they can move into the fourth phase, which is accepting the transition for what it is. Letting go may be a gradual 'three steps forward – two steps back' type of process. Someone who has been divorced may feel he or she has let go until they see their ex-spouse with a new partner. This may be quite painful and makes them think 'This is awful, I thought I was through this but I'm not'. Through the first three phases, there has been a kind of attachment, whether it has been conscious or not, to the past situation. To move from phase three to phase four involves a process of unhooking from the past and of saying 'Well, here I am now; here is what I have; I know I can survive; I may not be sure of what I want yet, but I will be OK; there is life out there waiting for me.' As this is accepted as the new reality, the person's feelings begin to rise once more, and optimism becomes possible.

'Let it happen: this is it' Have I felt like this? When?

....

....

5 Testing

The person becomes much more active and starts testing himself or herself in the new situation, trying out new behaviours, new life styles, and new ways of coping with the transition. After divorce this is often a stage when people begin dating again. There is also a tendency at this point for people to stereotype, to seek categories and classifications for the ways that people react to the new situation. There is much personal energy available during this phase and it sometimes shows itself in irritation, or tears.

'Perhaps if I try . . .' Have I felt like this? When?

....

....

6 Search for Meaning

Following the burst of activity and self-testing, there is a gradual shift towards understanding, when the person may ask, 'Is this right for me?' or 'What does this mean for me?' We need to know the meaning of these changes for us: how they will affect our future and our whole sense of who we are. If it is not 'right for me' then there will be further testing of alternatives until one is found that is right and fits with our sense of ourselves. It is only when we have a sense of what these changes mean, and what their meaning for our life is, that we can move on to the next stage.

'Is this right?' Have I felt like this? When?

....

....

7   Internalisation

At last, if the transition has ultimately been one we have accepted, we move into the final phase of internalising all the meanings and incorporating them into our changed behaviour, or routines, or life-style. The person who, on being made redundant, continues to leave home at the same time each morning and return the same time each evening is having difficulty with this final stage. In fact, they are having difficulty with the whole transition.

They may be stuck at the denial stage, or looping round between denial and self-doubt because they cannot yet accept the new reality. Acceptance is crucial before they move forward to the final stages of transition and the restoration of self-esteem. When we have fully accepted (internalised) the stages of change we have been through, then we can begin to look forward in a more positive frame of mind and start to build on the new strengths we have developed.

'Now I can see the way ahead' Have I felt like this? When?

....

....

Rarely, if ever, does a person move neatly from phase to phase. For example, one person may never get beyond minimisation or denial. Another may just stop at depression. Yet another might experience a major setback just as things begin to look up and revert to a less active phase. But for a transition to be effectively managed, we believe all seven phases have to be worked through. Often we try to avoid the depression stage, or help others avoid it, to prevent our own embarrassment, or to cover up our feelings of inadequacy. When we allow ourselves to grieve we can move towards the new opportunities opened up to us by the transition.

When we do allow ourselves to move forward, and finally reach the stage of internalisation, it can be like a rebirth, or an emergence from a long, dark winter into the bright light. We can feel like the brand-new butterfly which has metamorphosed over the months from a pupa into a splendid bright creature in a new world of freedom.

Understanding the stages of transition will help you to cope with your feelings and move forward. Think of a transition that you have experienced – it could be a move to a new school or neighbourhood, a change in a relationship, a change of occupation, or some other personal change that you remember.

Use the more detailed graph which follows to remind yourself of each of the seven stages. Make some notes on it to see if your transition fits in with these stages and the changes in self-esteem which accompany them.

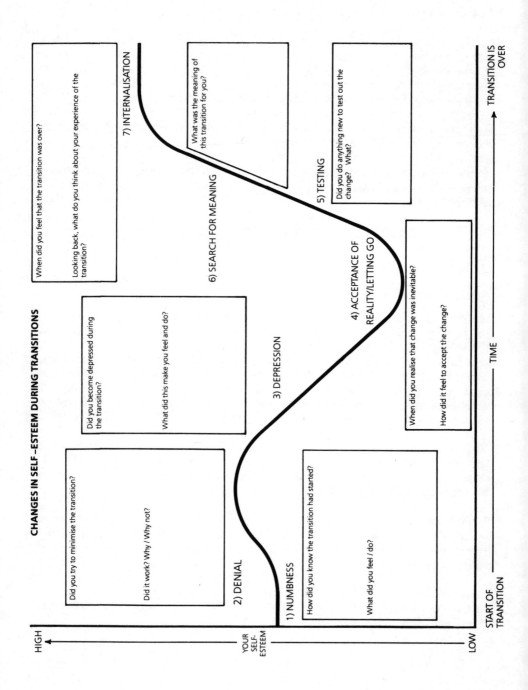

CHANGES IN SELF–ESTEEM DURING TRANSITIONS

HIGH

YOUR SELF-ESTEEM

LOW

1) NUMBNESS

How did you know the transition had started?

What did you feel / do?

2) DENIAL

Did you try to minimise the transition?

Did it work? Why / Why not?

3) DEPRESSION

Did you become depressed during the transition?

What did this make you feel and do?

4) ACCEPTANCE OF REALITY/LETTING GO

When did you realise that change was inevitable?

How did it feel to accept the change?

5) TESTING

Did you do anything new to test out the change? What?

6) SEARCH FOR MEANING

What was the meaning of this transition for you?

7) INTERNALISATION

When did you feel that the transition was over?

Looking back, what do you think about your experience of the transition?

START OF TRANSITION

TIME

TRANSITION IS OVER

Give your transition a name. Did it fit in with the pattern?

....

....

Each time you are invited to think about a transition you will be given a space to write down the name you give it. Later in the book there is a more detailed plan for dealing with a major transition. Reflecting on your past experiences will help you to prepare for this.

Summary

You are now aware of the seven stages:

- numbness
- minimisation
- depression
- acceptance of reality
- testing
- search for meaning
- internalisation.

You know that these are common features of transitions and your knowledge may help you to move more smoothly through the process next time. Like all skills, it takes practice. We are not suggesting, for example, that you can by-pass the stage of depression simply by knowing it exists, but at least you needn't feel guilty as well – you can work on overcoming the depression rather than covering it up.

Section Three: Some of Your Finest Transitional Moments

This section is wholly practical. It might take you several hours, or the remembrances of things past may stay with you over several days. We think that's OK. However, if at all possible, find an appropriate space in your life before you tackle this section. You now have an opportunity to relive in more detail some transitions you have experienced. This will build on your understanding of the seven stages of a transition and will enable you to understand how you respond to change.

You have already thought about some of the transitions you have experienced; now dig deeper into your memory to make a fuller list. Rather than trying to dredge items from an unwilling memory, use some of the following ideas to take you back. Try to find time to indulge yourself in this activity. The ultimate benefit to you might be very great.

Pictures of the Past

Get out your old photo albums and browse through them. Think about the kinds of transitions that were taking place. Look at old cine films or videos.

Swalk

If you keep old letters read through a few. What did people say to you? How have things changed? Look through your old diaries.

The Rock 'N' Roll Years

Listen to the music you used to enjoy at different stages of your life.

The Places we Went

Go somewhere you used to go. If you haven't been there for a while there will be plenty of opportunity to say 'It's all changed', and to think how *you* have changed.

The People we Knew

Reminisce about the good old/bad old days, if possible with others who were there.

Personal Project: My Life Plan – Past, Present and Future

Using these reminiscences and maybe some others, try filling in the Life Plan on the next page. Note down all the reminiscences you can possibly think of. Remember to include the Stages of Personal Development as well as Major Life Events. This is a long activity, so allow at least ten minutes for it.

The folllowing example should give you some ideas for your own Life Plan.

Margaret's Life Plan, as she approaches 50:

1 . . . . 2 . . . 3 **10** . . 4 . . . 5 . . 6 **20** . 7 . . 8 . . 9 . **30** . 10 . . . 11 . . 12 . **40** . . 13 . . 14 . . 15 **50** **60**

  1   My birth!
  2   Started school – I loved my first teacher, Mrs Jones.
  3   Birth of my sister. That put my nose out of joint for a while! Seems I was jealous and used to hide her so my mum couldn't find her!
  4   Went to big school. Hated it at first; it was so huge. Made good friends eventually. Wonder what happened to them?
  5   Left school.
  6   Started work in local accountant's office.
  7   Got married – parents not happy at first.
  8   Birth of first child – Lisa.
  9   Birth of James.
10   Moved to new house.
11   Returned to work.
12   Both parents died within six months. Had a terrible time: coping with full-time work, running a home and going to look after them every day. Lived with father and nursed him for the last fortnight.
13   Found a better job.
14   Children starting to leave home: Lisa is married and is working; James is a student.
15   Where I am now? What next? I suppose I have to get used to an empty house and decide whether to develop this new job into a career – that's one transition. Then there will be retirement, possibly weddings and grandchildren – that's a whole series of changes coming up.

You can see that Margaret's Life Plan raises a whole series of questions for her. What happened to those childhood friends? Will the departure of her children mean she has more leisure time? Should she use some of this time to trace those old friends or make new ones? Will her job be as fulfilling and demanding as raising a family? Or will she have time for new hobbies and activities? What should she do to plan for the changes ahead?

Now do your own Life Plan. Mark all your transitions on the timescale and make notes in the spaces provided below.

0 .... 10 .... 20 .... 30 .... 40 .... 50 60

AGE   NOTES

0–5

....

....

6–10

....

....

11–15

....

....

16–20

....

....

21–25

....

....

26–30

....

....

31–35

....

....

36–40

....

....

41–45   ....

....

46–50   ....

....

51–55   ....

....

56–60   ....

....

(There will still be transitions after 60, so continue on another sheet of paper if you wish.)

How many transitions have you marked on your Life Plan?

....

How many are stages in personal development (which everyone experiences) and how many are major life events?

....

Which transitions do you feel good about?

....

Which transitions were difficult for you?

....

Did anything surprise you?

....

What was your most interesting discovery?

....

How do you react to looking at your own Life Plan and your transitions?

....

....

....

Now choose two of the transitions that were important to you. Try to choose two with different characteristics; for example, one you felt good about and one that involved change that was difficult, or you were reluctant to accept. We shall use the experiences that you have gained from these two transitions to find out how you can build on your strengths to cope with future transitions. Give a name to each transition that you have chosen.

My two transitions are:

1 ....

2 ....

Look at each one in detail by noting down some answers to the following questions. Use your photos and your recent reminiscing to help you recall. Also apply the seven stages of a transition to remind you how you might have felt.

Transition 1 – My name for it

....

....

What do I remember?

....

....

....

How was I different afterwards from before?

....

....

Did it cause me any difficulty?

....

....

Did anything or anybody help? If so, how?

....

....

When did I feel comfortable again and accept the new situation?

....

How do I feel about that transition now?

....

....

Transition 2 – My name for it

....

....

What do I remember?

....

....

How was I different afterwards from before?

....

....

Did it cause me any difficulty?

....

....

Did anything or anybody help? If so, how?

....

....

When did I feel comfortable again and accept the new situation?

....

How do I feel about that transition now?

....

....

By considering these two transitions you have started to build up a picture of how you deal with change.

Make a note here of any characteristics you can recognise in your response to transitions.

Characteristics of my response to transitions are: ....

....

....

You might have noted that you are generally optimistic about life's changes or that wariness is always apparent in your early stages. We suggest noting them in case there are characteristics you would like to build on or change. The next section goes into this in greater detail.

Summary

Now you know how you have responded to transitions in the past, and maybe what is happening to you at the present time. You may feel that your past responses have been healthy, maybe not.

Section Four: Taking the Upset Out of Upheaval

This section will help you to clarify how you cope with transitions, and we will give you some suggestions so that you can develop these and other skills to enable you to take the upset out of upheaval.

We look at and suggest how you can:

- know what you want

- know your new situation

- know who can help you

- look after yourself

- leave the past behind.

Learning to Cope

Here are some questions about how you cope with transitions. Think about your own coping styles and your way of life and then apply the questions to one of the transitions you thought about in the last section (use the transition you think is most characteristic of your coping style).

Knowing What I Want

Is this transition something I want to happen?

....

Am I somebody who 'makes things happen' rather than one who sits back and lets things happen? Do I know what I want and make efforts to achieve it?

....

....

Do I know what I would like to get out of this new situation?

....

....

Do I know what I do not want from this new situation?

....

....

If I feel under stress, do I know what I can do to help myself?

....

....

If you answered 'Yes' to a question then you are obviously coping well with that area of the transition. If you answered 'No' you might find some of the ideas below helpful. (Even a 'yes' answer might get new ideas). Try to develop so that you can answer 'Yes' to more questions – then you will be well on the way to coping competently with transitions.

Knowing Myself Better

Often we do not choose transitions. This sometimes makes it difficult for us to accept the change, but basically we have only three choices:

- refuse to accept it

- accept it, but just 'put up' with it

- accept it and try to benefit from it.

The first will bring nothing but bad feelings and is unlikely to reverse the changes; it will probably mean that we are unable to cope with the tasks facing us in the new situation. The second will help us survive. The third will help us not only to survive but to benefit and grow from the experience.

It sometimes helps you to face your fears by asking 'What is the worst thing that can happen?' Our anxieties are usually based upon generalised, unidentified and fantastic fears. Actually facing up to the worst that can happen may help us to identify specific possibilities. If we think and talk about these possibilities, we will probably find that they are not that terrible, or that they are unlikely to materialise. Even if the worst does happen, at least we have prepared ourselves for it.

'Making things happen' in the way you want them to, rather than waiting for things to happen to you, is being *proactive*. It is an approach which believes that you can always make things 'more like you want them to be'; that you can be more 'in charge' of yourself and situations; that you and others can gain from being more self-directing; that you can be someone who does things for yourself rather than someone who has things done to you. It is not about being aggressive or ruthless, but rather more about choosing, acting and growing positively. The more you are thinking, deciding and doing for yourself the more useful you are going to be to yourself, to others and to society.

How proactive am I?

Answer these questions as honestly as you can.

Could I make a decision like the ones shown in the cartoon?

....

Do I spend a long time worrying about decisions?

....

Do I rely on other people to make decisions for me?

....

Do I keep my worries to myself?

....

Do I know how to help myself deal with decisions?

....

Just looking at your answers will tell you if you are satisfied with your ability to handle decisions or not. All change involves making decisions: sometimes easy, sometimes painful. Letting other people make decisions for you does not help you to manage your own transition and grow in the ways that you want. However, there are a number of things you can do which can help you be more proactive and feel more in control.

Try the following useful guidelines for a start:

- Look after yourself.
- Manage your transitions one at a time.
- Don't blame yourself or punish yourself.
- Manage decisions one at a time – or decide not to make a decision!
- Avoid over-complicating the issue by trying to deal with too many things at once, or avoid situations where you feel stressed and might over-react.
- Always remember that time will help as you progress through a transition though the more you can do actively to help yourself, the better.

It is worth looking at each of these in more detail. The following activities will help you identify ways in which you can help yourself if you are facing a transition or if you are in the middle of one now.

Look After Yourself

To begin with, answer the following questions.

Do I get regular exercise or have a keep-fit programme?

....

Do I eat regularly and sensibly?

....

Do I have a regular routine?

....

Do I have places to go to, people to be with, or comfortable situations which give me a secure base?

....

Do I give myself treats if I'm going through a bad patch?

....

Do I have people who will take care of me at times when I need them?

....

Am I able to 'survive' during hard times until better times come?

....

Do I know the times and situations when I am likely to be at my lowest?

....

When I feel low, do I do any of the following?

skip meals
cut exercise
forget my daily routine
sleep badly, or not long enough
avoid friends
neglect myself

If you have ticked any of the items on this list, then think carefully about the advice that follows. Looking after ourselves is the first and most important practical step we can take towards helping ourselves to deal with change.

Personal Project

Make a start by filling out the following simple timetable of a week's activities. Start by marking your most basic routines – times of going to bed and getting up; meal times; other regular activities such as going to work.

Now put in any regular exercise times. If you normally walk the dog each morning, mark the time that this occupies. If you attend an exercise class, or do your exercises at home each lunchtime, mark it in. Be truthful – the timetable should show a typical week's activity; it will not be useful to you if you are kidding yourself. Exercise is often one of the first casualties at times of stress!

Using a different colour, now mark in the times when you are normally relaxing. Include anything that you feel helps you to relax, from gardening to reading or watching a favourite TV programme. By the way, sitting in front of the telly, biting your nails and worrying does *not* count as relaxing!

Now take a little time to think of a typical week from better times in the past, when things were going well, a time when you felt on top of things, when every day was a good day. Would that week's timetable be very different? Are you taking less exercise? Spending less time relaxing? Skimping on meal times?

This timetable shows an eighteen hour day – which should be enough for most of us, bearing in mind that most of us need about eight hours' sleep a night. Mark your own hours at the top, so that, if you are a shift worker, for example, your day might run from 4 am to 10 pm. Using different colours for each activity (listed below) will help you see what you do when.

MON																		
TUES																		
WED																		
THURS																		
FRI																		
SAT																		
SUN																		

SLEEPING □ MEALS □ EXERCISE □ TRAVELLING □ RELAXATION □ OTHER ROUTINE □

Our ability to cope with stress depends on our physical well-being. We need to be fit and well to cope effectively with transitions, so exercise and eating regularly and wisely are essential coping skills. It is particularly important to eat well during a transition when you may have neither the time nor the inclination to do so.

Using the timetable, and your knowledge of yourself, write down the bad habits you fall into in times of stress. For instance, do you start drinking more alcohol in the hope that it will relax you? Do you find yourself snacking between meals when you are not really hungry?

....

....

....

What can you do to avoid these bad habits? What can you do to eat and drink more sensibly?

....

....

....

You could get a book on exercise and healthy eating to help you motivate yourself. Join a gym or exercise class. If you feel particularly unfit, see your doctor for advice on how to get fit.

What other things could you do to stay healthy and well?

....

....

Relaxation techniques are also well worth learning, as they can help prevent you from becoming too uptight about things that are bothering you. Make a point of spending a little time relaxing each day. It sometimes helps to give yourself a treat – an outing to a favourite, peaceful spot; a visit to the hairdresser, or to a friend; or buying yourself something small that you will enjoy.

What other things could I do to relax?

....

....

....

Exercising is a good way of relaxing and taking your mind off things. Squash, walking, swimming, yoga – almost any form of exercise will promote both physical and mental relaxation. Other ways of relaxing include gardening or DIY – anything which will take your mind off your problems.

Routine and structure in one's life can be of great assistance at times of transition. If our internal world is in disarray, then keeping our external world in order can help. Look for the 'anchor points' in your life, the zones of stability which you can be sure of while all else is changing. These range from the most basic of routines, such as going to bed at a regular hour, to mundane rituals like meals, shopping and work outside or in the home. The daily routine of delivering the children to school, for example, and meeting the teachers, the ritual exchange of greetings and news with other parents at the school gate, these are trivial events but can be a lifeline during difficult periods.

Recognise these daily routines and, instead of looking upon them as irksome, regard them as helpful anchor points in your day. Make a start with a new timetable now (a new one is provided on the next page) and mark each of these routines on it. This time, think about how to make these routines work for you: if your bedtime changes every day, think of the most sensible time to get to bed to ensure you get enough rest, and decide to make it a ritual.

Give your new timetable a heading: write on it 'How I Can Help Myself'. Now look at your answers to the questions about exercise, eating and relaxation. Make space on your timetable for your new ideas on eating well, exercising regularly and relaxation.

Knowing Others Who Can Help

Here is another set of questions to answer:

Who can I depend on in a crisis?

....

Who can I discuss my concerns with?

....

Who do I feel close to?

....

Who can recognise my strengths and make me feel valued?

....

MON						
TUES						
WED						
THURS						
FRI						
SAT						
SUN						

SLEEPING □ MEALS □ EXERCISE □ TRAVELLING □ RELAXATION □ OTHER ROUTINE □

Who can give me any information I need?

....

Who will challenge me and make me face up to things if I need to do so?

....

Who can I share good times and good experiences with?

....

There is now considerable evidence to show that talking problems through with people (friends, peers, parents, colleagues, even strangers) helps to reduce stress at times of change. Having a support group is a valuable asset. Your own support group could include your husband or wife, colleagues, a mentor, parents, relatives, friends. You can use this list of questions as a starting point when you come to consider where help is available, and the importance of developing a range of 'helpers' rather than being dependent on just one or two people for everything.

Obviously, most of our support comes from friends or those sympathetic to us, but it is also important to be challenged. Someone who can make us face up to things can actually provoke us into examining our ideas and actions in a very positive way.

The kinds of support I need:

....

....

....

....

People who can provide me with this support:

....

....

....

....

Is there a space in your timetable where you could plan to make contact with a friend, by visiting them, telephoning or inviting them out? Why not mark it in? All too often, at times of stress, we cut ourselves off from friends who could be most helpful. An evening out with a friend is relaxing and helps restore your sense of self-esteem at a time when you might need it.

Plan: Don't be Rushed

Manage your transitions one at a time

This might be easier said than done, as some major life events may involve several kinds of transition. For example, a move to a new home can also mean, as well as the search for suitable accommodation, adapting to new patterns of travel, finding new centres for shopping and leisure, a new job, and making new friends and contacts.

It will help you if you can identify each transition and deal with each separately, one at a time. It will not help you if you feel pressured into hasty decisions simply because of the sheer amount of change going on. If possible, take these major changes one at a time. This might mean planning ahead, so that you have time to settle into a new home and surroundings before you start the search for a job or a new school for the children.

Have you experienced times when many transitions were going on? How well did you cope?

....

Don't blame yourself or punish yourself

When things go wrong, as they are bound to sometimes, don't waste time in destructive self-criticism. This just undermines your self-esteem even further. Take time out to think about the new situation and how best to deal with it; give yourself a little treat to boost your self-esteem and you will be surprised how much easier it is to deal with whatever you feel has gone wrong.

Are you prone to self-blame? What can you do next time to avoid it?

....

Manage your decisions one at a time

It is surprising how many decisions can be safely postponed until you feel better able to make them. This is not the same as letting events or other people make your decisions for you, or dodging the whole issue and putting it off indefinitely. Rather, it is the clever knack of recognising which decisions have the highest priority and must be dealt with *now*, and which decisions can safely wait until you have more information, or until a decision has become absolutely necessary.

Don't let other people push you into making a decision you do not feel ready to make. If necessary, tell yourself and other people that you are busy dealing with another decision which must come first, and that you will deal with the next one when *you* are ready.

Do you experience the feeling of being overwhelmed by too many decisions at once? What can you do to deal with this problem in future?

....

You could make a list of all the decisions you need to make on one piece of paper, and then write it out again, but this time in order of priority.

Avoid over-complication and over-reaction

The same advice applies in this case too, with the added ingredient of stress: if you feel harassed by a particular situation and pushed into making a decision you don't feel you can make at that time, then avoid it or defuse it by simply saying, 'I am not going to make a decision on this right now. I will let you know when I have made my decision.' This straightforward approach helps other people to recognise your right to make your own decisions as and when you are ready.

Can you recognise when you are feeling stressed and sidestep or defuse the situation?

....

Remember that time will help

Time will help you come to terms with any new situation. But in order to come through a transition feeling that you have learned from the experience, you need to help yourself along the way (remember the person who got stuck at the stage of denial?). All of the reading and the thinking that you are doing now will help you to manage change in a proactive way – for yourself.

What has been the most important thing you have learned, or fully understood, for the first time about your own experience of transitions so far?

....

....

....

....

Summary

In this section we have looked in some detail at useful techniques for coping with difficult decision-making during times of transition. Perhaps you already use some of these techniques, but can now recognise when you are using them and why. If these techniques are new to you, don't wait for a major life event to try them out! Start putting them into practice straight away. Practise on the simple decisions is good preparation for the hard ones! In either case, you should be more aware of how you generally cope with decisions and change – and better equipped to be proactive about both in future.

Section Five: The Challenge of Change

All of the things that you have learned so far, like looking after yourself and creating a support network, will help you deal with future change.

How else can you prepare yourself for the transitions that lie ahead? One of the keys is to recognise when you are coming up to a transition so that you can prepare yourself. The second is to know in advance what you want out of the new situation.

Knowing my New Situation

What shall I call the new situation?

....

Do I know how I will be expected to behave in the new situation?

....

....

Is there any way that I can try out the new situation in advance?

....

....

What do I hope for out of the new situation?

....

....

What things can I do to be more aware of what I want from the new situation?

....

....

Talk to friends, or other people who are aware of your situation, about what you might expect to gain or lose. Discuss ways in which you can manage the change so that it goes the way you want.

Think forward to what the new situation will be like. Collect as much information as you can about the new situation: what will be expected of you? What is regarded as normal in this situation? What do others expect? This will give you a chance to ask:

Will I need to change in any way?

....

....

Do I want to change in any way?

....

Am I prepared to change in any way?

....

If the answer to the last question is 'No', you should examine your motives for refusing to change. As all transition involves change of some kind, it is important to accept change and make it work in the way you want. Some people find it difficult to accept change because of their attachment to their old situation. Is this you?

Leaving the Past Behind

Do I hang on to what is past or easily leave one situation and move to another?

....

Do I often think 'It's not fair. This should not happen to me!'?

....

Do I want to get through the bad patches, leave the past behind and carry on with what lies ahead?

....

Am I able to find opportunities to express anger or other strong feelings in ways that help?

....

Sometimes we think, feel, talk and act in a way which 'locks' us into a situation which we liked or in which we were secure and comfortable. We don't want to move, we just hang on. Hanging on to one situation, whether physically, psychologically or emotionally, can prevent growth and development.

There are a number of ways we might respond to leaving the past behind. We can:

- Wish it hadn't passed – but it has!

- Remember the good things – but they are gone and if we spend too much time remembering, we are missing new opportunities now and in the future.

- Refuse to think or talk about it – this probably means we are a slave of the past and not the master. Talking about the good and the bad can free us to move on.

- Not express our feelings of sadness, anger or whatever – unexpressed feelings are again likely to control us or block off future opportunities.

- Recognise that something good has gone. Appreciate it, talk about it, but leave that stage behind for the next.

What can I do to ensure that I leave the past behind in a positive way?

....

....

....

Of course there is another reason for reluctance to change – fear of the future. And because we cannot know for sure how things will work out, this uncertainty is one of the major features of any transition. But you can prepare yourself both to deal with the uncertainty and to reduce it. As we have seen throughout this workbook, many aspects of transition have both a positive and a negative side: they can be alarming, but also exciting.

The Chinese have two words for crisis: one means 'danger', the other 'opportunity'.

All transitions, however unwelcome, offer the prospect of growth and development. Few would choose unemployment yet it offers the opportunity for a personal re-evaluation. Many exciting new businesses have been started by people who saw this as the only way of breaking out of unemployment.

Transitions are challenging; it is only by responding to challenges that we realise our full potential, that we really achieve what we are capable of.

Personal Project: Seeing the Transition Positively

We ask you here to think again about the transition you used at the beginning of the last section. Then write down as many points as you can come up with in the two columns. However, before you enter an item in the DON'T LIKE column you must put one in the DO LIKE column.

Things I like (or might get to like) about the transition	Things I don't like about the transition

Hopefully, you have come up with some positive aspects of the transition. Usually when we stop ourselves being negative and force ourselves to be positive we can see the good in situations. Now answer these questions; they should encourage you to come up with even more positive ideas.

If you find it difficult to think of positive aspects of your transition, discuss it with someone else; perhaps they may see it from a different angle.

What is one thing that I hope to gain (or have gained) by moving into my new situation?

Transitions

What opportunities do I now have, which I didn't have, or hadn't thought of before?

....

....

....

Is there something new which I have learned about myself?

....

....

In what ways am I different now from how I was before?

....

....

....

....

Even if you find it difficult to see any new opportunities ahead, remember all the ways in which you can influence change, by acting proactively, for yourself. When you are facing the prospect of a transition in your life, at the time of maximum uncertainty, that is the time to start reducing the uncertainty, by planning to do those things that will help you. Remember your timetable of 'Ways in which I can help myself'? The anchor points and the helpful routines? The importance of rest, exercise and good food? Make a time plan here of when you could start to make the changes.

This week I will:

....

....

....

....

Starting day:

....

This month I will:

....

....

....

....

Starting day:

....

Next month I will:

....

....

....

....

Starting day:

....

In a year I will be better at:

....

....

....

....

Summary

Remember those Chinese symbols for crisis: one means disaster, the other means opportunity. Bear them in mind when you face times of transition, and concentrate on making the most of the opportunities presented to you.

If change is inevitable, then it is important that you know how to deal with leaving the past behind and facing the uncertainty of the future. You can develop ways in which you can help yourself to manage the transition smoothly and positively. With your new plans to look forward to, we will consider the challenge of change in the next section because, as we have been saying throughout, transitions aren't all bad – far from it.

Section Six: Your Next Transition

We have told you all we think you need to know about making transitions. Hopefully, as you worked through the book, you will have discovered that you knew most of it already: now you should be able to apply it.

To enable you to do that, this section invites you to think ahead. Anticipate change that you may face in the near future: perhaps you are thinking about marriage, working overseas, or some other change. Take this opportunity to plan how to ease yourself through the difficult stages and ultimately to benefit from the challenge.

Personal Project

We invite you now to take your time, reflect on what you have learned from this workbook, and complete this quiz, which asks you to comment on your feelings and your expectations before this expected transition.

Feelings and Expectations Before The Event:

Am I anxious about anything?

....

Am I excited about anything?

....

What am I looking forward to?

....

What will I miss?

....

What do I know about the new situation? What have I done to try to find out?

....

Will there be any difficulties? If so, what?

....

Is there anything I can do now to prepare? If so, what?

....

....

....

What help will be available if I need any? (Use this space to write a list of your anchor points, the people in your support group, treats you could give yourself, etc.)

....

....

....

....

....

....

....

....

....

....

....

Transition Chart

Use the boxes on the chart on the next page to show the events that you think will occur at each of the seven stages of the transition (this way, you will be prepared for the low point in your self-esteem and it will not take you by surprise).

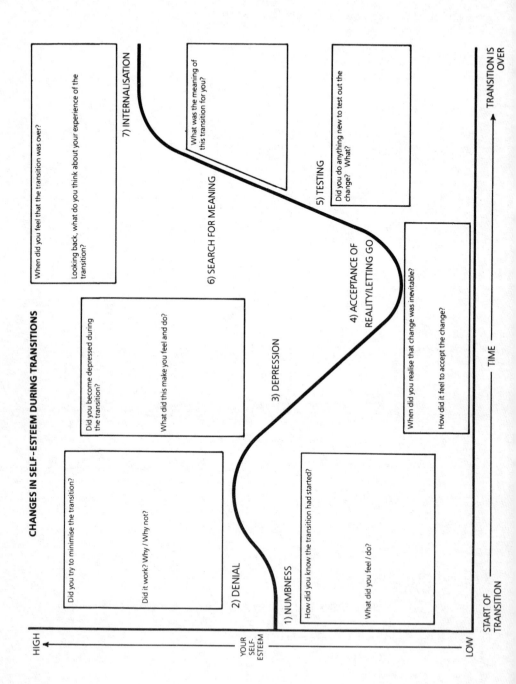

CHANGES IN SELF-ESTEEM DURING TRANSITIONS

HIGH

YOUR SELF-ESTEEM

LOW

START OF TRANSITION

TIME

TRANSITION IS OVER

1) NUMBNESS

2) DENIAL

3) DEPRESSION

4) ACCEPTANCE OF REALITY/LETTING GO

5) TESTING

6) SEARCH FOR MEANING

7) INTERNALISATION

Did you try to minimise the transition?

Did it work? Why / Why not?

Did you become depressed during the transition?

What did this make you feel and do?

When did you feel that the transition was over?

Looking back, what do you think about your experience of the transition?

What was the meaning of this transition for you?

Did you do anything new to test out the change? What?

When did you realise that change was inevitable?

How did it feel to accept the change?

How did you know the transition had started?

What did you feel / do?

Just having thought about your next transition will help you to deal with it. When your next transition actually occurs, use this table to keep a record of your feelings during it.

Keep this safe to use during the next transition.

Transition Record

Fill in the seven stages chart and the table as you progress through the transition. Analysing what happens as it happens will not only help you with your next transition, but with all your future transitions.

On-Going Record During Transition:

Feelings: 1. at the start	
2. after one day	
3. after two days	
4. after one week	
5. later (say when)	
6. later (say when)	
How did you behave: at each of above stages	(1)
	(2)
were you restless, relaxed, anxious, etc?	(3)
	(4)
	(5)
	(6)
Difficulties encountered: By you	
By others	
How you coped	
How you saw others cope	

Coping Techniques:

Try each of these, if appropriate, and note whether it helps or not.	
1. Discuss how you feel with somebody. Does it help?	
2. Find somewhere quiet to relax. Does it help?	
3. Try thinking about the way things were prior to the transition. Does it help?	
4. Try some physical activity, e.g. exercise, gardening, decorating, etc. Does it help?	
5. Try thinking of all the best things about the new situation. Does it help?	
6. Try giving yourself a treat – something your really enjoy. Does it help?	
7. Anything else you found helpful?	

Moving Through The Transition:

When did you begin to feel relaxed, 'at home' or adjusted to the new situation?	
How long had the transition lasted?	
What had helped you to feel at home?	
Had you done anything to help yourself?	
Had others done anything to help you?	
Are there any differences between: (i) what you expected and (ii) what actually happened	

What the Transition Taught Me.

What did I learn about myself?

....

....

About other people?

....

....

About moving into new situations in the future?

....

....

Congratulations! Another milestone in your life has been passed. We hope you have gained from it.

Summary

Having planned carefully for your next transition will help you to move through it more easily. You will be more likely to expect the unexpected, you will be ready for the low points in your self-esteem, and you will concentrate on the opportunities presented by the transition.

Section Seven: Helping Others

Everyone goes through transitions, and by now you have some expertise in the field. If you know someone who is having difficulty with a transition, you may be able to help them. Here are some of the things you could do:

- **Listen to them Talk** about the transition, try to bring out their feelings about it.

- **Suggest**, sensitively, some of the strategies for coping with transitions that you think will be useful.

- **Give them a Treat** – even better than getting them to give one to themselves.

- **Offer Practical Help**.

Anything else you can think of:

....

....

Do you know anyone going through a transition? If so, who?

....

How can you help them?

....

....

....

When will you help them?

....

Not only will helping someone else make you feel good, there's also a chance they'll help you out in the future.

One Final Comment: Metamorphosis

When a chrysalis metamorphoses into a butterfly it is a natural process, it is something that must happen for the insect to become beautiful, to be able to fly, to realise its potential.

This is a good symbol for us when we face transitions because for us to realise life's potential we need to change, and change is inevitable. Even so, it often causes us stress and worry.

Having worked through this book we hope you will have developed the following knowledge and skills:

- You are able to recognise a transition and whether it arises from a major life event or a stage of personal development.

- You know that there are seven stages through which you must pass in a transition: numbness, minimisation, depression, acceptance of reality/letting go, testing, search for meaning, internalisation.

- You can apply the above to transitions in your own life.

- You are aware of the stress you may face during a transition and you now have ways of coping with it.

- You now that transitions present opportunities for you to make the most of.

- You have skills which enable you to handle transitions well.

Use this knowledge and these skills whenever you face a difficult transition and, as you already know, things will become easier.

Lifeskills

Personal Development Series

Other titles available in this series are:

TIME MANAGEMENT:
Conquer the Clock

Time Management is about recognising that time is limited, setting clear priorities and objectives for yourself, and then ensuring that you achieve them. *Conquer the Clock* will:

- show you how to analyse your present use of time, including the concept of sold, maintenance and discretionary time

- help you identify the priorities in your life and rank them in order of importance

- introduce you to the many different ways and styles of managing time.

COMMUNICATION:
Time to Talk

'It is tempting to assume that our communication skills come to us as part of our natural development. Yet some people develop into very effective communicators, while others barely reach survival level.' Without communication there would be no relationships between people: sharing ideas, giving opinions, finding out what we need to know, working out differences, giving positive criticism and expressing our feelings are examples of the kind of face-to-face communication which is essential to our everyday life and work with other people. *Time to Talk* will:

- explain how to recognise and prevent 'communication breakdown' at work and at home
- help you to identify helpful and unhelpful ways of communicating
- encourage you to develop and improve your interpersonal communication skills.

ASSERTIVENESS:
A Positive Process

'When we are assertive, we tell people what we want or need, or would prefer. We state our preferences clearly and confidently, without being aggressive, without belittling ourselves and without putting other people down.' Most of us are capable of being assertive, aggressive or unassertive at different times. The aim of this book is to help you benefit from the positive process of being assertive as consistently as you can. *Assertiveness: A Positive Process* will:

- help you to distinguish between assertive, aggressive and unassertive behaviour

- ensure that you understand the benefits of being assertive – and the dilemmas

- introduce you to some helpful techniques for dealing with people assertively.

Other Mercury titles from Lifeskills are:

BUILD YOUR OWN RAINBOW
Barrie Hopson and Mike Scally

A Lifeskills Workbook for Career and Life Management

Adopted by the Open University for Work Choices, a Community Education course.

Build Your Own Rainbow is the first of a new series of Lifeskills guides. It contains 40 exercises that will help answer the questions:

- who am I?
- where am I now?
- how satisfied am I?
- what changes do I want?
- how do I make them happen?
- what if it doesn't work out?

In the process of doing this, readers will discover what is important to them about work, where their main interests lie, what their transferable skills are and which career pattern would best suit them. They will be helped to set personal and career objectives, to make action plans and to take greater charge of their lives.

12 STEPS TO SUCCESS THROUGH SERVICE
Barrie Hopson and Mike Scally

A Lifeskills Management Guide

Satisfying the customer is the single most vital factor in business success and the main priority in any business must be to win and keep the customer. This book provides a complete programme to achieve success through service in twelve crucial steps:

- decide on your core business
- know your customer
- create your wisdom
- define your moments of truth
- give good service to one another
- manage the customer's experience
- profit from complaints
- stay close to your customer
- design and market the service programme
- set service criteria
- reward service excellence
- develop the service programme.

Lifeskills is one of the leading providers of Quality Service Programmes in the English-speaking world.

POSITIVE LEADERSHIP
Mike Pegg

How to Build a Winning Team
A Lifeskills Management Guide

Good leaders have many features in common. They develop a clear vision, they inspire their people, gain commitment from them, then guide their teams to success. This sounds easy in theory, but how is it done?

This is a book written for top teams, managers, and anybody who is a leader of people. It offers a framework for leadership and teamwork, with concrete ideas which can be incorporated into the daily work plan.

If focuses on how to:

- provide positive leadership
- be a positive team member
- build a positive culture
- set a positive goal, and get commitment to reaching it
- be a positive implementer
- build a positive reputation
- get positive results
- continue to build a positive and successful team.